MW00932450

This Journal Belongs To

Jarslie Publishing – jarlsie.com

Made in the USA
Las Vegas, NV
08 October 2023

78760717R00072